D0673145

BACK OF THE THROAT

BY
YUSSEF EL GUINDI

★

DRAMATISTS
PLAY SERVICE
INC.

BACK OF THE THROAT
Copyright © 2006, Yussef El Guindi

All Rights Reserved

SPECIAL NOTE

SPECIAL NOTE ON SONGS AND RECORDINGS

For my mother

AUTHOR'S NOTE

A few suggestions: Try to make sure the actor playing Khaled keeps it light and welcoming for as long as he can. Refrain from playing Khaled too indignant or fearful for at least a quarter of the play — up until he first opens the door and asks them to leave. And even then, he's still trying to be civil. As are the agents. The longer we can keep it "civil," the better. The more the humor, grounded, will come out, and prepare the audience for when the tension increases. Yes, Khaled is anxious, but I think the character is working to overcome that. I've noticed that if the audience sees Khaled as being under the gun too soon — sees that he's fearful — they will become fearful and anxious on his behalf, and the humor will be squashed.

For the same reason, the agents need to be genuinely civil, and real, and not come off as caricatures. I.e., we can't give the audience an out, a way to dismiss the agents as not real. It also helps if the actor playing Carl has a sense of comic timing. (Actually, that applies to all the actors, except perhaps for Asfoor.)

For the very same reason, keep the pre-show music and/or sound effects "light" in the sense of avoiding creating discomfort/tension in the audience as the lights go down. This is by way of suggesting that a play as tone-sensitive as this is going to be spun one way or another by something as mundane as pre-show music/sounds. (In regards to sound: The entrance of Asfoor should be accompanied by some sort of sound effect. Past productions have used the sound of an airplane flying by. Also, the tail end of Asfoor's last speech, at the end of the play — or right after he finishes — has often been under-scored by music or sounds. This is optional, but can be effective. It could also just be an ominous rumbling sound that comes in.)

Pacing: Keep the play moving. Especially as we enter the second half of the play, with the entrance of Asfoor and Shelly, etc. Stitch these two halves together by maintaining the energy and drive of the first half when we only have Carl, Bartlett and Khaled onstage.

Handling the violence: It is a shift in the play, and the more you can smooth that transition, the better. Be careful not to go over the top and badger the audience too much. It's a little bit like shouting onstage. Too much of it can be off-putting … And when Carl does his number on Khaled, it is important that the actor playing Khaled modulate his pained reactions. Yes, be real, but don't go over the top in terms of conveying the physical pain of Khaled; otherwise, again, it will push the audience away.

Finally, in a couple of productions, I found myself acting as Khaled's lawyer, defending his innocence. It's important for the actor playing Khaled to move forward with a sense of his character's innocence. Having said that, the ending is intentionally ambiguous. Perhaps this encounter actually took place. (In which case the agents have good cause to feel Khaled is a "person of interest," if not more.) Or, it is a mental/emotional projection of Khaled's. Either way, the idea with the ending is to say that innocent or guilty, Khaled will forever be associated with Asfoor and the attacks, and that nothing he can do or say will ever clear him.

BACK OF THE THROAT was co-produced by Thick Description (Tony Kelly, Artistic Director) and Golden Thread Productions (Torange Yeghiazarian, Artistic Director) in San Francisco, California, opening on April 18, 2005. It was directed by Tony Kelly; the set design was by James Faerron; the costume design was by Isabella Ortega; and the lighting design was by Rick Martin. The cast was as follows:

KHALED .... James Asher
BARTLETT .... James Reese
CARL .... Paul Santiago
SHELLY/BETH/JEAN .... Chloe Bronzan
ASFOOR .... Brian Rivera

BACK OF THE THROAT was produced at Theater Schmeater (Rob West, Artistic Director) in Seattle, Washington, opening on May 19, 2005. It was directed by Mark Jared Zufelt; the set design was by Corey Ericksen; the lighting design was by Lynne Ellis; the costume design was by Colleen Gillon; and the sound design was by Maurice "Mo" Smith. The cast was as follows:

KHALED .... Alex Samuels
BARTLETT .... Chris Mayse
CARL .... Erik Hill
SHELLY/BETH/JEAN .... Kate Czajkowski
ASFOOR .... Johnny Patchamatla

BACK OF THE THROAT was produced at Manbites Dog Theater (Jeffrey Storer, Artistic Director) in Durham, North Carolina, opening on November 3, 2005. It was directed by Jay O'Berski; the set design was by David Fellerath and John Galt; and the lighting design was by Lionel Mouse. The cast was as follows:

KHALED .... Bart Matthews
BARTLETT .... David Berberian
CARL .... Jeffrey Scott Detwiler
SHELLY/BETH/JEAN .... Dana Marks
ASFOOR .... Ken Wolpert

BACK OF THE THROAT was produced at Cyrano Theater Company (Sandy Harper, Artistic Director) in Anchorage, Alaska, opening on January 6, 2006. It was directed by Dick Reichman; the set design was by Doug Frank; the costume design was by Kris Root and Company; the lighting design was by Kris Root; and the sound design was by Erick Hayden. The cast was as follows:

KHALED .... Brandon Lawrence
BARTLETT .... Dean Williams
CARL .... Mark Stoneburner
SHELLY/BETH/JEAN .... Veronica Page
ASFOOR .... Bowen Gillings

BACK OF THE THROAT was produced at the Flea Theater (Jim Simpson, Artistic Director; Carol Ostrow, Producing Director) in New York City, opening on February 2, 2006. It was directed by Jim Simpson; the set design was by Michael Goldsheft; the costume design was by Erin Elizabeth Murphy; and the lighting design was by Benjamin C. Tevelow. The cast was as follows:

KHALED .... Adeel Akhtar
BARTLETT .... Jason Guy
CARL .... Jamie Effros
SHELLY/BETH/JEAN .... Erin Roth
ASFOOR .... Bandar Albuliwi

BACK OF THE THROAT was produced at Silk Road Theatre Project (Jamil Khoury, Artistic Director; Malik Gillani, Executive Director) in Chicago, Illinois, opening on April 4, 2006. It was directed by Stuart Carden; the set design was by Lee Keenan; the costume design was by Janice Pytel; the lighting design was by Kurt Ottinger; and the original music and sound design were by Robert Steele. The cast was as follows:

KHALED .... Kareem Bandealy
BARTLETT .... Sean Sinitski
CARL .... Tom Hickey
SHELLY/BETH/JEAN .... Elaine Robinson
ASFOOR .... Madrid St. Angelo

BACK OF THE THROAT was produced at Furious Theatre Company (Brad Price, Sara Hennessy, Eric Pargac, Vonessa Martin, Shawn Lee, and Damaso Rodriguez, Artistic Directors) in Pasadena, California, opening on June 24, 2006. It was directed by Damaso Rodriguez; the set design was by Shawn Lee; the costume design was by Rachel Canning; the lighting design was by Dan Jenkins; and the sound design was by Cricket Strother Myers. The cast was as follows:

KHALED	Ammar Mahmood
BARTLETT	Anthony Di Novi
CARL	Doug Newell
SHELLY/BETH/JEAN	Vonessa Martin
ASFOOR	Aly Mawji

CHARACTERS

KHALED
BARTLETT
CARL
ASFOOR
SHELLY
BETH
JEAN

Note: Shelly, Beth and Jean are
to be played by the same actor.

SETTING

Khaled's apartment.
Sometime after the attacks.

The play is performed without intermission.

BACK OF THE THROAT

Khaled's studio. Futon on floor. Assorted objects, furniture. Bartlett stands opposite Khaled. Carl is flipping through a book. He will continue to methodically inspect other books, papers, as well as clothes.

BARTLETT. We appreciate this.
KHALED. Whatever you need, please.
BARTLETT. This is informal, so —
KHALED. I understand.
BARTLETT. Casual. As casual as a visit like this can be.
KHALED. Either way. Make it formal if you want. I want to help. I've been looking for a way to help.
BARTLETT. Thanks.
KHALED. Horrible.
BARTLETT. Yes.
KHALED. Horrible.
BARTLETT. Nice space.
KHALED. Yes. — A little claustrophobic. But it's cheap.
BARTLETT. Live simply, they say.
KHALED. I'd live extravagantly if I could afford it.
BARTLETT. What's this say? *(Bartlett picks up a picture frame from a table.)*
KHALED. A present from my mother ... It says, er, "God."
BARTLETT. "God"?
KHALED. Yes.
BARTLETT. It's pretty.
KHALED. It is ... I'm not religious myself.
BARTLETT. I've always been impressed with this ... *(Makes a motion over the writing with his finger.)*
KHALED. Calligraphy?
BARTLETT. Very artistic. Why the emphasis on — calligraphy? I see it all the time.

KHALED. Well — frankly — I'm not sure its — I know in general that, the religion tends to favor abstraction to, er, human representation. The idea being to avoid worship, or, too much distraction with the, um, human form … In truth I don't know a whole lot about it.

BARTLETT. No television?

KHALED. No. Too addictive. It's easier to remove the temptation.

BARTLETT. *(Picking up a book.)* You didn't see the images?

KHALED. Oh yes. God, yes. How could I not? I wish I hadn't. *(The tinkling of a tune is heard. Khaled and Bartlett turn in the direction of Carl, who is standing holding a music box. A beat as they all stand and listen to the tune.)*

CARL. "Oklahoma"?

KHALED. I've never been able to identify the tune.

BARTLETT. *(Referring to the book.)* And what's this about? *(Carl closes the music box and places it next to another object he's selected. He resumes his search.)*

KHALED. It's the, um — Koran.

BARTLETT. Huh. So this is it.

KHALED. Another present from my mother. Her idea of a subtle hint.

BARTLETT. *(Flips through book.)* You're not religious, you say?

KHALED. No. She is.

BARTLETT. Didn't rub off.

KHALED. Unfortunately not.

BARTLETT. Why "unfortunately"?

KHALED. Well — because I hear it's a comfort.

BARTLETT. And if you had to sum up the message of this book in a couple of lines?

KHALED. Er. The usual. Be good. Or else.

BARTLETT. Sounds like good advice to me. How come you're not religious? *(Khaled looks over at what Carl is rifling through.)*

KHALED. I was never comfortable with the "or else" part.

BARTLETT. Nobody likes the punishment part.

KHALED. I'd like to think God isn't as small-minded as we are.

BARTLETT. I guess the point is there are consequences for our actions. Funny, huh. How a book can have such an impact.

KHALED. Yes. I was just reading about Martin Luther and the Reformation and how the whole —

BARTLETT. *(Interrupting.)* Am I pronouncing that correctly? "Kaled"?

KHALED. Close enough. *(To Carl.)* Is there anything in particular you're looking for?

BARTLETT. Don't mind him. He's just going to do his thing.

KHALED. But if there's anything —

BARTLETT. *(Interrupting.)* With your permission, if we still have that.

KHALED. Go ahead, but if there's something —

BARTLETT. *(Interrupting.)* "Kaled"?

KHALED. Er, Khaled.

BARTLETT. "Haled"?

KHALED. More Khaled.

BARTLETT. "Kaled."

KHALED. That's good.

BARTLETT. But not exactly.

KHALED. It doesn't matter.

CARL. Khaled.

KHALED. That's it.

BARTLETT. It's that back of the throat thing.

KHALED. Right.

BARTLETT. Carl spent some time in the Mideast.

KHALED. Oh yes?

BARTLETT. So how do you stay informed then? With no TV. Newspapers? The internet?

KHALED. Both.

BARTLETT. And when you want to kick back, you...?

KHALED. *(Not getting what he means.)* When I...?

BARTLETT. How do you relax?

KHALED. Well ...

BARTLETT. How do you spend your free time?

KHALED. Really? That's relevant? *(Bartlett stares at him.)* Er, sure, okay. I read, mostly.

BARTLETT. Uh-huh.

KHALED. That's my big thing, reading.

BARTLETT. And when you want to amuse yourself, you do what?

KHALED. *(Referring to the books.)* Actually I find that stuff amusing.

BARTLETT. *(Holding up a periodical.)* This stuff?

KHALED. Some of it.

BARTLETT. *(Reading the cover.)* *Wheat Production and the Politics of Hunger*?

KHALED. A real page turner.

BARTLETT. *(Pointing to the computer.)* Can we look at that, by

13

the way?

KHALED. It's kind of private. *(Slight beat.)* It's — kind of private. *(Carl and Bartlett are looking at Khaled.)* Will you be taking it away?

BARTLETT. I doubt we'll need to look at it.

KHALED. If you want to.

BARTLETT. I'm actually more curious about how you kick back. What you do when you want to relax. Break your routine. Spice things up.

KHALED. Can I ask how that helps you? Knowing how I amuse myself?

BARTLETT. The questions will seem a little intrusive, unfortunately. There's no avoiding that.

KHALED. I understand. I just don't have that exciting a life. Did I mention I'm a citizen, by the way. I can show you my — *(Carl holds up Khaled's passport.)* Right. Just so you know. *(Carl puts it among two or three other items. This pile will gradually grow.)*

BARTLETT. Here's the thing. We know you're bending over backwards and I sense we're going to be out of your way shortly.

CARL. Be done in five.

BARTLETT. And we know you didn't have to let us do this.

KHALED. Are you looking for anything in particular? Maybe I can just point you to it.

BARTLETT. He's just going to poke around. It's a random thing.

KHALED. Are you sure? The strange thing is I was going to call you. A friend of mine said he would, which made me think I should too.

BARTLETT. Who?

KHALED. Er — a friend?

BARTLETT. Right; and that friend's name?

KHALED. *(Hesitates.)* Hisham. He wouldn't mind me telling you.

BARTLETT. Hisham what?

KHALED. Darmush. He was thinking of calling you too.

BARTLETT. I look forward to hearing from him.

KHALED. I thought maybe I should just to let you know I'm — here, you know. I am who I am and — just so you're not wondering — in case my name comes across your desk which it obviously has. I wish you'd tell me who gave you my name.

BARTLETT. Also know that anything you say here will be held in strict confidence.

KHALED. *(Continuing.)* Because then maybe I could address the concerns head on; so you don't waste your time. I imagine you're getting a lot of calls. People with scores to settle. Or skittish neighbors. Was it George? He seems a little too curious about where I'm from. He doesn't seem to understand my connections with my country of birth are long gone. Was it — Beth? We had a falling-out. It's very strange not being able to address whatever accusations have been made against me. It's like battling ghosts.

BARTLETT. I didn't say anything about accusations.

KHALED. There haven't been? *(Bartlett stares at him; slight beat.)* Er, amuse myself? Let's see, I go to movies, I read. I like eating out; I sit in cafes. I like to go for long walks. I feel like I'm writing a personals ad. I wish there was more to tell. You'll leave here thinking, gee, what a lame life this guy leads.

BARTLETT. That's the other thing: If you have nothing to worry about, then you have nothing to worry about. I know a visit from us can be unsettling. It's an awkward part of this job that when we come around people aren't necessarily happy to see us. We've held meetings to see if we can't fix that, but I guess there's no avoiding the fact that this is what it is. I'm a government official, uninvited, and you've been yanked out of your routine.

KHALED. You're more than welcome, I assure you.

BARTLETT. And we appreciate that.

KHALED. I've wanted to help.

BARTLETT. What I'm saying is we know we've put you on the spot.

KHALED. Well —

BARTLETT. *(Continuing.)* It would be natural to be ill at ease, regardless of whether you want us here or not.

KHALED. Sure.

BARTLETT. *(Continuing.)* Don't waste time trying to appear innocent if you are. If you're innocent, you're innocent. You don't have to work at it.

CARL. *(Turning around, to Khaled.)* "Karafa."

KHALED. What?

BARTLETT. So relax.

KHALED. I'm trying.

BARTLETT. We're not here to get you for jaywalking. Don't worry about us finding small stuff. We all have small stuff we'd rather not have people see.

KHALED. Not even that. That's what I'm saying, I'm not even hiding any interesting, non-political stuff.

BARTLETT. Stuff like this. *(From under a pile of magazines, he picks out a porn magazine.)* Don't worry about this stuff.

KHALED. Okay. That.

15

BARTLETT. It's not a big deal.

KHALED. It's — sure.

BARTLETT. *(Flipping through magazine.)* Not a huge one anyway.

KHALED. It's legal.

BARTLETT. It's porn. Not good. But it's still okay.

KHALED. They haven't outlawed it yet.

BARTLETT. No, but that doesn't make it all right.

KHALED. It's — it's a debate, but sure.

BARTLETT. A debate?

KHALED. Er, yeah.

BARTLETT. A debate how?

KHALED. About — you know — the place of erotica in society.

BARTLETT. Uh-huh … You think this is healthy? *(Shows Khaled a picture.)* With cows?

KHALED. I don't much care for the farm theme, no.

BARTLETT. You think this should have a place in society?

KHALED. It already does have a place in society.

BARTLETT. So does murder. Doesn't make it okay.

KHALED. I'm not sure I'd equate that with murder.

BARTLETT. You go for this stuff? On the kinky side?

KHALED. What's kinky? She's draped over a cow. It's actually meant to be an anti-leather kind of thing. If you read the blurb. A cow wearing a human. A reverse sort of — vegetarian's point of view of sex and fashion. It's a stretch. But someone in that magazine is obviously an animal rights person. Or is pretending to be for the sake of something different.

BARTLETT. The woman doesn't seem to fare too well.

KHALED. No, but — What does this have to do with anything? It's one magazine. *(Carl holds up four or five more porn magazines.)* Yes. I'm allowed.

BARTLETT. Careful there. You don't want to get caught in little lies over nothing.

KHALED. What lie? I thought you didn't care about the small stuff.

BARTLETT. I don't. It's just a pet issue I have.

CARL. *(To Khaled.)* "Hany-hany."

KHALED. I'm sorry: Am I supposed to understand that?

BARTLETT. You don't speak Arabic?

KHALED. No. That's why I didn't call. I knew you were looking for Arabic speakers. *(Carl holds up two books in Arabic.)* Yes. I keep telling myself I should learn it. Look, I hope you're not going to pick apart every little thing because I'm sure you could come to all sorts of conclusions by what I have. As you would with anyone's home. Come to a bunch of false conclusions by what someone has. Which may mean nothing more than, you know, like a Rorschach test. Without taking anything away from your training; but still: a porn magazine, Arabic books? So what?

BARTLETT. Uh-huh.

KHALED. It's my business. — I don't have to apologize for it. Do I?

BARTLETT. No, you don't. Or any of these titles. *(Carl hands him a few of the books he selected.) Getting Your Government's Attention Through Unconventional Means, A Manual for the Oppressed, Theater of the Oppressed, Covering Islam, Militant Islam. (Holds up a little red book:) Quotations from Chairman Mao Tsetung?*

KHALED. I'd heard so much about it.

BARTLETT. Do you feel that oppressed?

KHALED. I was a lit major; I read everything.

BARTLETT. And so on. *(He throws the rest of the titles on the futon.)* It's not what we care about.

KHALED. Good, because on the face of it I know —

BARTLETT. *(Interrupting.)* On the other hand a person is reflected by what he owns. It'd be silly to deny that. If you walked into my home, or Carl's, you'd find us. In what we did and didn't have. Just as you are here in all this.

KHALED. But — context is everything. Otherwise, yes, some of this I know looks suspicious. I've played this game myself: walked into my studio and wondered what it might say about me; seeing if something would make me out to be something I'm not.

BARTLETT. You're surrounded by the things that interest you.

KHALED. I have a book on assassins, what does that mean? I bet you've seen it and a red flag's gone up.

BARTLETT. What does it mean?

KHALED. Nothing. If I found that book in your home, what would that mean?

BARTLETT. It would mean in my line of work it would make sense to study the topic. What does it mean for you?

KHALED. I'm a writer; I read lots of things, for just in case — in case a plot line requires an assassin. I have a book on guns which I'm sure you've selected. *(Seeing it.)* Yes, you have. I actually hate guns but finding that you might think gee, okay, here we go.

BARTLETT. Why do you have a book on guns?

KHALED. I told you, I'm a writer. I need any number of reference books on different subjects. That's the context.

BARTLETT. Okay. Now we know. That's why we have to ask. We have no way of knowing unless we ask. Which means throwing our net pretty wide. Please try not to get worked up in the process.

KHALED. I'm not.

BARTLETT. We're not here to unravel your personal life beyond what we need to know.

KHALED. It just feels this isn't as casual as you make it out to be. You're here for something specific, obviously, something brought you to my door. My name came across your desk and I wish you'd tell me why. If you allowed me to clear that up, maybe you could get on with finding the people you really want. *(Bartlett and Carl stare at him.)* I mean I appreciate the effort you're making, but I just sense something's being left unsaid and I would really like to address whatever that is. It's like this itch you've brought in that I wish I could just scratch, for all our sakes.

BARTLETT. Huh. Itch.

CARL. *(Removes his jacket.)* Can I use your bathroom?

KHALED. It's right through there.

CARL. "Shukran." *(Carl exits.)*

BARTLETT. No, right, it's probably not as casual as I'd like it to be. Though we have begun training sessions on that very subject, strangely, even for old-timers like me. "How to put people at ease." I didn't do too bad at it.

KHALED. No, you're — I am at ease.

BARTLETT. Thank you. In fact: *(Takes out a form from his pocket.)* If I can have you fill this out at the end of this, I'd appreciate it. It's an evaluation form. And then just mail it in. We're trying to get direct feedback from the public. Especially from our target audience.

KHALED. I'd be happy to.

BARTLETT. And if you could use a Number 2 pencil.

KHALED. Sure.

BARTLETT. So yes, we try, but at the end of the day, there's no getting around the intrusiveness of all this: What am I doing here? A government official, in your home, going through your stuff and asking you questions.

KHALED. I'd love to know that myself.

BARTLETT. And that's what we'll find out. But in the meantime there's no avoiding the fact that that's who I am. Engaged in trying to find out who you are.

KHALED. I wish there was a way of showing you that I'm nobody interesting enough to have you waste your time.

BARTLETT. And you might not be.

KHALED. I'm not; how can I show you that?

BARTLETT. Well, that's the thing. How can you show me that?

KHALED. Is there anything in particular you want to know?

BARTLETT. Is there anything you'd like to tell me?

KHALED. If you told me what brought you here —

BARTLETT. *(Interrupting.)* How about the computer? Anything I might want to see?

KHALED. No. Unless you want to look at a bunch of half-finished stories.

BARTLETT. Half-finished?

KHALED. Most of them.

BARTLETT. Why?

KHALED. "Why?"

BARTLETT. Writer's block?

KHALED. Sometimes.

BARTLETT. How come?

KHALED. It's an occupational hazard. It happens.

BARTLETT. Something going on to make you lose focus?

KHALED. Apart from the world going to hell?

BARTLETT. That inspires some people.

KHALED. Not me.

BARTLETT. It inspires me to do the best I can.

KHALED. Well, good.

BARTLETT. What inspires you, if I can ask?

KHALED. I never know ahead of time, that's why it's an inspiration.

BARTLETT. We know some of your interests, right, politics, sex.

KHALED. Not even that. But then, doesn't that cover most people's interests?

BARTLETT. I wouldn't say that. No. You wouldn't find these books in my house.

KHALED. Still, they're pretty basic, whether you have a direct interest in them or not.

BARTLETT. They're basic if you consider them important, otherwise they're not.

KHALED. To be an active, informed citizen? And to have a healthy interest in, in — sex; that's not normal?

BARTLETT. No. No, this isn't normal. I have to tell you, Khaled, none of this is normal. Right about now I would place you a few feet outside of that category. *(Khaled looks dumfounded.)* To be honest, you are shaping up to be a very unnormal individual. I am frankly amazed at just how abnormal everything is in your apartment. I have actually been growing quite alarmed by what we've been finding. More: I'm getting that uncomfortable feeling that there's more to you than meets the eye and not in a good way. I wouldn't be surprised if we were to turn on that computer and find plans for tunneling under the White House. Or if Carl was to walk out that door having found something very incriminating indeed.

KHALED. You're — joking.

BARTLETT. I try not to joke before drawing a conclusion. It takes away from the gravity of the impression I'm trying to make. *(The toilet flushes.)* Carl. Are you done in there?

CARL. Just washing my hands.

BARTLETT. Can you hurry up, please.

CARL. I'll be right out.

KHALED. What happened to being casual?

BARTLETT. Oh, we're done with that. Could you turn on your computer, please.

KHALED. I — I think I'd like to, er … speak to a lawyer.

BARTLETT. Ah. Uh-huh.

KHALED. I — don't know what's going on anymore.

BARTLETT. I think you do is my hunch.

KHALED. Yuh. Okay. I think I'd like to speak to a lawyer if you don't mind.

BARTLETT. I do mind.

KHALED. I have the right.

BARTLETT. Not necessarily.

KHALED. Yes, I believe I do.

BARTLETT. I'd have to disagree.

KHALED. I know my rights.

BARTLETT. What you do have is the right to cooperate with your intelligence and do the right thing and asking for a lawyer is a dumb move because it alerts me to a guilt you may be trying to hide. Which further suggests that I need to switch gears and become more forthright in my questioning; which usually means I become unpleasant. Which further irritates me because I'm a sensitive enough guy who doesn't like putting the screws on people and that makes me start to build up a resentment towards you for making me behave in ways I don't like … I am perhaps saying more than I should, but you should know where this is heading.

KHALED. *(Taken aback.)* I'd … I'd like you to leave, please.

BARTLETT. I'm sorry you feel that way.

KHALED. I'm sorry too, but I — I think that's advisable. If there's something specific you want me to address, then fine. But. And in that case I would like to have a lawyer present. But I no longer wish to be subjected to this — whatever is going on here, so please. *(He gestures towards the door.)* I'd appreciate it if you — and then if you want me to come in, I'll do so willingly with a lawyer.

BARTLETT. Er, Khaled, you can't have a lawyer.

KHALED. Yes, I can, I know my rights.

BARTLETT. No, you don't, you've been misinformed. Could you switch on your computer, please?

KHALED. I don't have to do that.

BARTLETT. Yes, you do, because I'm asking nicely.

KHALED. *(Moves towards the phone.)* I'm — I'm calling a lawyer.

BARTLETT. Is it smut you're trying to hide?

KHALED. No.

BARTLETT. Weird fantasies? Child porn?

KHALED. No!

BARTLETT. Child porn with domestic pets involved?

KHALED. What?

BARTLETT. So then it must be something to do with, what? dicey politics? military info? blueprints? communiques with the wrong people?

KHALED. *(Overlapping.)* No. What are you — ? None of that. No; that's —

BARTLETT. I mean we've already established you're a left-leaning subversive with Maoist tendencies who has a thing for bestiality and militant Islam. Throw in your research on guns and assassins and I could have you inside a jail cell reading about yourself on the front page of every newspaper before the week is out.

KHALED. Is this — ? What — ? Are you trying to intimidate me? *(Bartlett stares at him.)* No. — Look, I — No. *(Goes to the phone and starts dialing.)* I don't know if this — if you're kidding me or — but. This isn't —

BARTLETT. Khaled.

KHALED. I don't know what's going on anymore. Something isn't …

BARTLETT. Put the phone down.

KHALED. I don't even know now if you're who you say you are. You could be a couple of con artists who walked off the street for all I know.

BARTLETT. Would you like to call our office instead?

KHALED. I would like you to leave.

BARTLETT. Okay, but put the phone down first.

KHALED. I'm going to call my friend who'll know who I should —

BARTLETT. *(Interrupting.)* PUT THE PHONE DOWN! *(Khaled puts the phone down. Slight beat.)*

KHALED. *(Quiet.)* I have rights. *(Slight beat.)* I do have rights. This is still — I don't have to show you anything if I don't want to unless you have a — which doesn't mean I'm trying to hide anything, it just means I care enough about what makes this country — you know — to exercise the right to say no. There is nothing on that computer that would interest you, I promise you. And even if there were, I still have the right to — *(Bartlett continues to stare at him.)* They're stories, okay, I told you. Still in progress. I'd rather not have people go poking around something that's still very private. It would be like opening a dark room while the photos are still developing. It would be a horrible violation for me. That may be —

BARTLETT. *(Interrupting, holds up his finger.)* Sorry: Khaled? Hold that thought. *(Goes to bathroom door.)* Carl. Could you stop whatever it is you're doing and come out please. *(The door opens and Carl emerges wearing a fatigue jacket and a baseball cap.)* Ah. Ah-ha.

CARL. I was searching the pipes.

BARTLETT. *(Re: the clothes.)* Well. There we go.

CARL. *(Re: the clothes.)* In the laundry basket, at the bottom.

BARTLETT. Really. Oh, well.

CARL. *(Holds up bottom of jacket.)* Evidence of nasty right here.

BARTLETT. *(Feels bottom of jacket.)* Yuck.

CARL. Smell it.

BARTLETT. I'll take your word for it.

CARL. Also — *(Takes out a swizzle stick.)*

BARTLETT. A swizzle stick.

CARL. And — *(Takes out a small piece of paper.)*

BARTLETT. A receipt. From. *(Reads it.)*

CARL. Guess where.

BARTLETT. Oh; wow.

CARL. Look at the date. *(Bartlett looks.)* Same date.

BARTLETT. Wow.

CARL. Proof positive.

BARTLETT. Looks like it.

CARL. He's our man.

BARTLETT. Uh-oh.

KHALED. What?

BARTLETT. Uh-oh.

KHALED. Why are you wearing that?

BARTLETT. You were where you shouldn't have been, Khaled; in a place you shouldn't have gone to. Bad news. Very bad news.

KHALED. What is — ? What does that — *(Re: the receipt.)* I don't even remember what that is. *(Khaled moves to look at it, but Bartlett gives the receipt to Carl, who pockets it.)*

BARTLETT. *(Taking off his jacket.)* As we shift a little here, I want to assure you of a few things: We will not overstep certain lines. We will not violate you or your boundaries in any way. Though we might appear pissed off, you are not to take it personally or feel this is directed at you per se. And though we may resort to slurs and swear words, the aggression is not focused on you so much as it an attempt to create an atmosphere where you might feel more willing to offer up information. *(Over the above speech, Carl has taken a chair and placed it in various spots — as if to see where they might best place Khaled.)*

CARL. Here?

BARTLETT. Anywhere. *(Back to Khaled.)*

KHALED. What are you doing?

BARTLETT. One more thing: At no time should you think this is an ethnic thing. Your ethnicity has nothing to do with it other than the fact that your background happens to be the place where most of this crap is coming from. So naturally the focus is going to be on you. It's not profiling, it's deduction. You're a Muslim and an Arab. Those are the bad-asses currently making life a living hell and so we'll gravitate towards you and your ilk until other bad-asses from other races make a nuisance of themselves. Right? Yesterday the Irish and the Poles, today it's you. Tomorrow it might be the Dutch.

KHALED. Okay — okay, look, look: You need to tell me what the hell is going on.

BARTLETT. We'll get to that. We're doing this as efficiently as we can.

KHALED. Because. I think. Actually, you know. *(Moves to the door.)* You need to leave. I'm sorry, but — er. I don't have to do this. And I, er, yeah. You need to go. *(Opens door.)*

BARTLETT. Khaled.

KHALED. You need to go.

BARTLETT. Don't be a party pooper.

KHALED. I would be happy to do this with a lawyer.

BARTLETT. Close the door. *(Carl moves towards Khaled and the door.)*

KHALED. You know what? I need to see your badges again because I'm not even sure anymore. *(Carl takes hold of the door and closes it.)* Can I see your badges again, please? Because. Whatever this is, this doesn't feel like it's, er, procedure. This is more like, you know, I mean, you're acting like a couple of, er, thugs, frankly. And I realize intimidation is part of the process, but this is — *(A nervous laugh perhaps.)* speaking of boundaries.

BARTLETT. Anything you don't like, you write it down on the evaluation form.

CARL. You gave that to him already? *(Searches his pockets for his form.)*

BARTLETT. I understand your getting nervous. I don't care for this part myself. We're switching from being civil and congenial to being hard-nosed and focused. It will have the effect of taking away from your humanity and it doesn't do much for ours. Plus we're trying new approaches. It's all new territory for us. Which is why we're handing out these forms.

CARL. Here we go. *(Hands form to Khaled.)*

BARTLETT. You don't like something, write it down. Even if we haul you into permanent lock-up, we're still going to pay attention to your feedback. We might get things wrong in the short term, overdo things, with the interrogation, etc., but our image, honestly, how we come across, that can't be our main priority right now.

KHALED. Interrogate me about what?

BARTLETT. Our image can't be more important than questions of safety.

CARL. We don't give a rat's ass.

BARTLETT. We do give a rat's ass. But is it more important?

CARL. *(Half to himself.)* No, obviously we give a rat's ass.

BARTLETT. You care about this country? Yes? You want it safe?

KHALED. But I haven't done anything and you're acting like I have, what have I done?

BARTLETT. What is more important: Inconveniencing you with accusations of having broken the law or ensuring the safety of everyone?

KHALED. But how am I a threat to that, I haven't broken the law!

BARTLETT. I'm speaking about in principle.

KHALED. Even in principle!

BARTLETT. I'm trying to be clear about this. I want the process to be transparent.

KHALED. I'm more confused than ever.

CARL. *(To Khaled.)* You look like you need to sit down. You're beginning to wobble.

KHALED. What?

BARTLETT. Would you like a glass of water before we start?

KHALED. Am I under arrest? *(Neither of them answer.)* Am I under arrest? Because if I'm not and you're not taking me in, then you need to — this is over.

BARTLETT. Khaled.

KHALED. You need to go. *(Goes to door.)* I know my rights. This is over. *(Opens door.)*

BARTLETT. Khaled.

KHALED. You bet I'll fill in those forms. This is — this is way over the line. Acting like some — cut-out pair of thugs playing tag to try and intimidate me. This is my country too, you know. This is my country! It's my fucking country!

BARTLETT. Khaled, the neighbors.

KHALED. I don't care if they hear it, let them hear it!

CARL. Not if you're guilty.

KHALED. I'm not guilty!

CARL. Then sit down and tell us about it.

KHALED. Tell you what? You haven't told me what I've been accused of!

CARL. Shut the door and we'll tell you.

KHALED. I'm not going to tell you anything until I have a lawyer present! This is still America and I will not be treated this way! *(Bartlett quickly walks over to Khaled, grabs him by the arm and drags him into a corner of the room — away from the door, which Carl shuts. Bartlett pushes Khaled into a corner and stands inches from him. While being dragged to the corner, Khaled says:)* What — ? What are you doing? Let go of me. Let go of me.

BARTLETT. First thing: Shut up.

KHALED. No, I —

BARTLETT. *(Interrupting.)* Second thing, shut up.

KHALED. No, I won't, I —

BARTLETT. *(Interrupting.)* If I have to tell you what the third thing is, I will shut you up myself. *(Khaled opens his mouth but is interrupted.)* I will shut you up myself.

CARL. *(Walks over to them.)* Listen to the man.

BARTLETT. And if I hear you say "this is still America" one more time I am going to throw up. I will open your mouth and hurl a projectile of my burger down your scrawny traitorous throat. Do you understand me?

KHALED. I'm not a traitor.

BARTLETT. Do you understand me?

CARL. Come on, man. Be cooperative.

BARTLETT. *(To Khaled.)* If I hear another immigrant spew back to me shit about rights, I will fucking vomit … You come here with shit, from shit countries, knowing nothing about anything and you have the nerve to quote the fucking law at me? Come at me with something you know nothing about?

CARL. *(To Bartlett.)* Easy, man.

BARTLETT. It pisses me off! … "It's my country." *This* is your fucking country. Right here, right now, in this room with us. You left the U.S. when you crossed the line, you piece of shit.

CARL. *(To Bartlett, quiet.)* Hey, hey.

BARTLETT. America is out there and it wants nothing to do with you.

CARL. Hey, Bart.

BARTLETT. It's galling. — Sticks in my craw. To hear these people who got here two hours ago quote back to me Thomas Jefferson and the Founding Fathers. They're not his fucking Fathers.

CARL. They become his Fathers. That's what makes this country special, man.

BARTLETT. I understand; but it's like they wave it at you like they're giving you the finger. *(Sing-song:)* "You can't touch me, I have the Constitution."

CARL. They do have the Constitution.

BARTLETT. I know that, Carl. I'm just saying it's galling to hear it from people who don't give a shit about it.

KHALED. I do give a shit about it.

BARTLETT. No, you don't.

KHALED. I do, very much.

BARTLETT. Don't lie to me.

KHALED. It's why I became a citizen.

BARTLETT. You became a citizen so you could indulge in your perverted little fantasies, you sick little prick. Come here, wrap the flag around you and whack off. *(He picks up a porn magazine.)* Well I don't particularly want your cum over everything I hold dear!

CARL. Hey, Bart. *(Takes Bartlett aside.)*

BARTLETT. *(To Carl.)* I don't!

CARL. I know, it's okay.

BARTLETT. Jesus. Goddamn it.

26

CARL. I know.

BARTLETT. It's plain to see and we dance around it. We tip-toe and we apologize and we have to kiss their asses.

CARL. Don't blow it.

BARTLETT. I'm not; but sometimes it has to be said.

CARL. Okay, but let's stay on topic.

BARTLETT. This is the topic.

CARL. The point of the topic.

BARTLETT. *(Beat; to Khaled.)* And I have nothing against immigrants. Let me make that clear.

CARL. *(Takes porn mag from him.)* Hear, hear.

BARTLETT. The more, the merrier. God bless immigrants. My great grandfather was an immigrant.

CARL. Mine too. Both sides. *(Carl will start leafing through the porn magazine.)*

BARTLETT. This country wouldn't be anything without them. God bless every fucking one of them. My family worked damn hard to make this country the place it is. And if you came here to do the same, I will personally roll out the red carpet for you. But if you've come here to piss on us. To take from us. Pick all the good things this country has to offer and give nothing back and then dump on us? … Then I don't think you're making a contribution, not at all.

KHALED. I am making a contribution.

BARTLETT. You're unemployed. You're on welfare.

KHALED. I have grants.

BARTLETT. That's taking.

KHALED. It's a prize.

BARTLETT. For what?

KHALED. For my stories.

BARTLETT. You haven't finished one.

KHALED. For past stories.

BARTLETT. You're blocked, you aren't writing, that means all you're doing is taking from the system.

CARL. *(Still leafing through the magazine.)* Leeching.

KHALED. I am writing, I'm just stressed out.

BARTLETT. You're involved in something you shouldn't be, that's why you're blocked. It's hard being creative when all you're thinking about is plotting destruction.

KHALED. I'm not, why are you saying that? *What are you accusing me of?*

CARL. The point is he doesn't have anything against immigrants.

Let's be clear about that.

BARTLETT. *(To Khaled.)* I'm dating an immigrant.

CARL. She gave you her number?

BARTLETT. *(To Khaled.)* This is not why I'm pressing down on you. Apart from the reservations I just spoke about, the best thing going for you now is that you are fresh off the boat.

CARL. *(Re: the girlfriend.)* You lucky bastard.

BARTLETT. If it turns out you're not involved in any of this shit, I will personally apologize and invite you out somewhere. In the meantime, why don't you show Khaled why he's neck-deep in doo-doo.

CARL. Love to.

KHALED. What?

CARL. *(Searches his pockets; to Bartlett.)* Hey, you know I met Miss September. *(Referring to the porn magazine.)*

BARTLETT. Who?

CARL. When I was helping the guys out on vice. Miss September. Just the nicest person. Devastated the attacks came on her month and ruined what could have been her big breakthrough. Was ready to quit until some guys wrote in saying how her body helped them through their darkest hours.

BARTLETT. *(Not amused.)* Great.

CARL. *(Reaches for his jacket.)* Now she only does spreads for special occasions. Usually to do with law enforcement.

BARTLETT. I don't really need to hear this.

CARL. *(Searches his jacket pocket.)* I'm just saying, funny, huh? You never know what gets some people through the night. For some it's like, you know, the church. For others — *(Finds what he's looking for.)* it's a place like this. *(He shows Khaled a photo.)* Ever been to this strip club? *(Khaled tries to focus on the photo.)* Well, we know you did because here you are in this photo. *(Shows him another photo.)* Hidden in this hat and jacket I'm wearing, but: Now that I'm wearing it we can pretty much say it's you. You can make out your jaw under the hat, and the earlobe is always a distinguishing feature. It's you, right? *(Khaled looks but doesn't answer.)*

BARTLETT. Khaled.

CARL. Plus we have your receipt from the club and a bunch of other stuff that places you there.

KHALED. Why are you — ? Why was this — ?

CARL. So it is you. *(Khaled hesitates.)* I would acknowledge the obvious so you can quickly move ahead and establish your innocence, if that's the case. Which is not obvious.

BARTLETT. It's far from obvious.

CARL. I'd use this opportunity to clear up your name, if I was you. *(Khaled is about to speak but is interrupted; sotto voce:)* And look, man, don't be embarrassed about going to these joints. I've frequented these places myself. I'm not as hung up about this as Bart here is.

BARTLETT. I'm not hung up about them.

CARL. What I'm saying is someone in this room understands.

BARTLETT. I understand. It was the cow that put me off.

CARL. Personally, you can whack off all you want. You can take your johnson and do what you want with it, as long as it's legal. We're not here to judge you for what you do with your dick. What's that expression in Arabic they use? About a fool and his schlong? Anyway. If you're just embarrassed to admit you go to strip joints, don't be. I love a good lap dance myself. That ass waving in your face. The thighs working up a sweat. *(Shows him the photo again.)* You, right?

KHALED. Look I … I don't know where you're heading with this. I'm not going to incriminate myself when I don't even know what I'm being accused of. You asked if you had my permission to come in here and everything, well, you don't anymore, I'm sorry.

BARTLETT. We're so past that, my friend. Right now you're standing on our permission not to be disappeared into little atom-sized pieces of nothingness; and then shoved up the crack of the fat ass you'll be sharing a cell with. The best thing you can do for yourself is to identify yourself right now, and I mean right now. *(Carl sticks the photo in front of Khaled's face.)*

KHALED. You can't tell anything. It's too dark. It's a silhouette for chrissakes.

BARTLETT. Then maybe we shed some light. Would that be helpful?

CARL. Shedding light is always a good idea.

BARTLETT. *(To Khaled.)* This is going to be like pulling teeth, isn't it? Carl.

CARL. I'm ahead of you. *(Carl goes over to the closet doors as he takes off the baseball hat and jacket.)*

BARTLETT. Exhibit number one. *(Shows Khaled another photo.)* Have you seen this guy? *(Carl slides open one of the doors, revealing Asfoor: erect, still. Perhaps a spotlight from within the closet is shone on him. Also helpful if a sound effect of some sort accompanies the opening of the door.)* Of course you have, he's been in all the papers. "Terribilis Carnifex," bringer of chaos, exemplar of horror and ghoulish behavior and very committed. And dead of course. Dying at the conclusion of his mad little goal. As a writer do you often wonder what might have been going through his mind at that instant he knew he'd accomplished his goal? Do you? I do. I wonder what he saw — just before he stopped seeing. What he thought, before he accomplished seizing everyone's mind and focusing it on him and his odious little ways. I admire him, you know. If I was an evil little shit, I'd want to be him. That's commitment for you. Dedication. *(To Asfoor.)* What did you see, by the way?

ASFOOR. Nothing.

BARTLETT. What did you think?

ASFOOR. Nothing.

BARTLETT. Unfortunately, I can't get into his mind. But he did do a lot of typing. *(Asfoor goes over to Khaled's computer. He will start typing.)* Quite the wordsmith. If a little cryptic. We've been able to trace most of his emails. Worked out of a library not too far from here. The librarian remembered him. Said he was like a dark cloud that changed the mood the moment he walked in. But said she felt sorry for him nonetheless. Reminded her of Pigpen, she said. *(Carl slides open the other closet panel revealing Shelly, wearing glasses.)*

SHELLY. Like in "Peanuts."

BARTLETT. Ah.

SHELLY. *(Enters studio.)* You know, the way he always had this cloud of dirt around him.

BARTLETT. I see.

SHELLY. That way. I thought it might be sadness at first, and felt the urge to say something to him. Cheer him up. *(To Asfoor.)* It's a wonderful day. We haven't had this much sun in weeks. *(Asfoor turns to her without saying anything.)* Have a nice day. *(To Bartlett.)* Didn't say much in return. No, I can't say he did. Barely smiled. His eyes were so … *(Can't find the words.)*

BARTLETT. Yes?

SHELLY. Piercingly nondescript. As if I was looking at a description of a pair of eyes, and not the eyes themselves. Of course all these impressions may be hindsight.

BARTLETT. What do you mean?

SHELLY. You know, how new information about a person suddenly makes you see that person in a different light. I'm sure if you'd told me he'd saved the lives of a family from a burning house I'd be remembering him differently. — Though probably not.

BARTLETT. Anything else?

SHELLY. Well ... *(Hesitates.)* He may have misread my attempts to be nice. Because one day he followed me into the room where we archive rare maps. And, well, made a pass at me. Didn't know he was there until I felt his hands. I screamed, of course. Pushed him away. I even had to use one of the rolled-up maps to ward him off. I kept thinking, I hope it doesn't come to anything violent because this is the only existing map of a county in eighteenth-century Pennsylvania.

BARTLETT. Why didn't you report the assault?

SHELLY. I don't know why I didn't. — I didn't want to give it — importance. Perhaps if I had, you would've caught him and none of this would have happened. I'm sorry. How do you recognize evil?

BARTLETT. We appreciate the information you're giving now.

SHELLY. All I saw was an awful sadness. I had no idea his hurt had no end.

BARTLETT. Thank you, Ms. Shelly. If we have any follow-up questions we'll contact you.

SHELLY. I wish ... *(To Asfoor.)* I wish you hadn't done that. I wish there had been a way to get to you earlier, before things turned; before your mind went away. Because it has to go away to do that, doesn't it? Become so narrowed that nothing else matters. — I wish I could talk to you. — I would even let you ... touch me, again. If it would open you up. If I could talk to you one more time; and find out more about you. Every day I walk into a building filled with more knowledge than I could ever hope to digest. But none of the books can explain to me why you did what you did or who you are ... I wonder if you'd even be able to tell me?

BARTLETT. Thank you, Ms. Shelly. Carl will show you out. *(With one last look at Asfoor, Shelly heads for the front door. Carl opens the door and exits with her.)* I don't suppose you've ever seen this man up close? *(Bartlett briefly picks up a library book.)*

KHALED. Because we used the same library?

BARTLETT. Locked eyes across a library table?

KHALED. That's the connection? It's the only library for miles, everyone uses it.

BARTLETT. *(Continuing.)* Rubbed shoulders in the bookshelves. Shared books? Emails?

KHALED. *(Overlapping.)* That's what brought you here? You don't think I wouldn't have come forward if I'd seen him, if I'd had any information about him.

BARTLETT. Perhaps you did and didn't know it; look at him again. *(He's shown the photo. At this point, if not before, Asfoor is up on his feet.)*

KHALED. I know what he looks like. I would've remembered.

BARTLETT. Look at him again.

ASFOOR. Khaled.

KHALED. You're not going to pin this on me just because I went into the same building.

ASFOOR. I'm bleeding into you and there's nothing you can do about it.

BARTLETT. Pin what?

KHALED. Jesus Christ, I've been wanting to help.

BARTLETT. *(Overlapping.)* Pin what? You may have seen him, that's all.

KHALED. I wept for this country.

ASFOOR. So did I.

BARTLETT. I'm trying to jog your memory, you may have forgotten something, seen him at the computer.

KHALED. I know what you're doing and I'm not going to be screwed by something this flimsy. I will not be dragged in by association of having used the same space!

BARTLETT. Khaled: Calm down; you aren't being accused of anything yet.

ASFOOR. We're all in this together.

BARTLETT. Perhaps you have some insight into this email he sent; it's translated.

ASFOOR and BARTLETT. "Nothing the matter today. On Wednesday, I cut myself opening a can of tuna. Don't worry about that. Do you know Luxor? It's worth seeing."

BARTLETT. Or —

ASFOOR. "Tattoos, yes. Do it where the skin folds so you can hide it if you change your mind."

ASFOOR and BARTLETT. "I have a list for you."

BARTLETT. Is "Luxor" part of your email address or how you sign off?

KHALED. No. "Luxor"? *(Pointing to the computer.)* Check it. This is like twenty degrees of separation. Then everyone in that library is a suspect. I use books, for chrissakes, I'm a writer.

BARTLETT. So you keep telling me.

ASFOOR. You're blocked, I can help.

BARTLETT. Ms. Shelly can't be definite she saw you two together, all the same she did say —

KHALED. *(Interrupting.)* How would she know who I am? *(Asfoor picks up a book.)*

BARTLETT. I showed her your photo.

KHALED. Where'd you get that?

BARTLETT. Your ex-girlfriend.

KHALED. *(Digests the information.)* How many people have you talked to exactly? What did Beth say?

BARTLETT. *(Consulting his notebook.)* But Ms. Shelly does think she saw him nearby when you came to ask for a book one time.

ASFOOR. *(Reads title of book.)* Caravans of God and Commerce.

BARTLETT. Remembers it because you kicked up a fuss when they didn't have it.

ASFOOR. *(Reading from book.)* "The road to Mecca was perilous, and not only because of the dangers of the desert."

BARTLETT. Says he stood a few feet away until you had finished and then followed you out.

ASFOOR. *(Reading from the book.)* "But also because of those who hid in them."

KHALED. What?

ASFOOR. *(Accent, to Khaled.)* Excuse me, sir.

KHALED. No.

BARTLETT. Said there may have been an exchange between you.

ASFOOR. *(To Khaled.)* I know book you want. I help you find it.

KHALED. That never happened. You don't think I would have remembered that? I'm a terrible liar. It would be obvious if I was lying. *(Asfoor has put down the book; Bartlett picks it up.)*

BARTLETT. I believe you. But you did find the book.

KHALED. In a book shop, I bought it.

BARTLETT. He never followed you out? Told you where you could find it?

KHALED. No.

BARTLETT. Perhaps the librarian did remember it wrong but if we speculated on this encounter that never took place, what might have happened?

KHALED. What kind of sense is that?

BARTLETT. He followed you out and …

KHALED. What am I supposed to speculate on?

BARTLETT. You're the writer, you tell me.

ASFOOR. *Assalam alaykum.*

KHALED. *(Disoriented.)* I can't remember what never happened.

ASFOOR. *Assalam alaykum.*

KHALED. *(Awkwardly.) Alaykum salaam.*

ASFOOR. *(In Arabic.)* I know that book you want.

KHALED. I don't speak Arabic.

ASFOOR. *(In Arabic.)* No?

KHALED. I'm sorry, I'm in a hurry.

ASFOOR. Please. A moment. I would like — my name is Gamal. Gamal Asfoor. Hello.

KHALED. Sorry, but I have to go.

ASFOOR. I like to learn English. With you.

KHALED. I — no, I'm sorry.

ASFOOR. You teach me. I pay.

KHALED. I can't. I'm really busy right now.

ASFOOR. *(Holds out a piece of paper.)* My number here. I teach you Arabic. You Arab, yes? I watch you. I watch you in the library.

KHALED. No thanks. Thank you, no, goodbye.

ASFOOR. I know book you want. I get it for you.

KHALED. Really, I can't. *(To Bartlett.)* That's ridiculous. There was no encounter. You're making stuff up.

BARTLETT. Well, of course I am. You of all people should appreciate the importance of doing that. How that might lead you, stumbling, to a truth or two. Facts aren't the only game in town. Perhaps it never happened, then again, here are the Arabic books. In this story we're making up, maybe he gave them to you.

KHALED. What kind of deductive leap is that? That's worse than guessing. *(Asfoor goes to sit at the computer.)*

BARTLETT. From his letters we know he shared similar interests with you: writing, poetry, Middle Eastern stuff, politics, radical books, porn, didn't much like women. Said some nasty things about women in his letters.

ASFOOR. *(At the computer.)* "Unclean."

BARTLETT. God knows what his childhood must have been like.

ASFOOR. "They corrupt. They diminish you. When I die, do not let them touch me."

KHALED. What on earth does that have to do with me?

BARTLETT. Well, Khaled, not knowing you; not really knowing much about you; just from meeting you and casual observance I would have to say your relation to the opposite sex seems to have a kink or two in it. *(Khaled looks at him, dumfounded.)* Maybe you two commiserated and found solace in the same twisted images and depictions.

KHALED. I don't know who you're talking about anymore; it's not me.

BARTLETT. I'm just saying.

KHALED. *(Overlapping.)* This is beyond making stuff up, this is *Alice in Wonderland.*

BARTLETT. Your girlfriend had a lot to say on the matter. *(A knock on the door.)*

KHALED. I knew it. She started this whole ball rolling, didn't she.

BARTLETT. I didn't say that, but she was helpful.

KHALED. She's the one who called you.

BARTLETT. The word "betrayal" came up a lot.

KHALED. *(Continuing.)* Something completely personal gets blown up because an ex holds a grudge. Great. *(There's another knock on the door.)*

BETH. *(Offstage.)* I'm coming. *(Beth enters from the bathroom in a bathrobe. She is drying her hair with a towel. Overlapping with this:)*

KHALED. You're going to take the word of someone who's pissed off with me? *(Beth has opened the door to Carl.)*

CARL. *(Shows her his badge.)* Good morning. Ms. Granger?

KHALED. *(Overlapping.)* For something completely unrelated?

CARL. I wonder if we could talk with you a moment.

BETH. What is this about?

KHALED. Jesus, talk about the personal being political; now she gets to drive home that point and nail me with it.

BARTLETT. *(Looking at his notebook.)* She said some interesting things right off the bat.

BETH. So he was involved after all.

CARL. What makes you say that?

BETH. Was he like one of those cells that get activated?

KHALED. She said that?

BARTLETT. Why don't you let me finish first?

BETH. That would make sense. His whole life seemed to be one big lie. I don't think he has an honest bone in his body. What did he do exactly?

CARL. We're just trying to get a better idea of who he is at this point.

BETH. When you find out let me know. Because I sure as hell didn't. You spend two years with someone thinking you have a pretty good idea of who you're shacking up with, then boom, he pulls some shit that makes you wonder who you're sleeping with.

CARL. Like what exactly?

BETH. And I like to think of myself as an intelligent person.

35

CARL. What in particular made you —

BETH. *(Interrupting.)* Just everything. He never seemed to come clean about anything. Always keeping things close to his chest, like he had another life going on. It wouldn't surprise me if he was involved. Though I can't imagine he was high up in whatever structure they have. I could admire him if he was. But he's too weak for that. More like a wannabe. Like someone who would be quite willing to take instructions, if you know what I mean.

CARL. I don't; can you explain that?

BETH. Like he knew his life was for shit and something like this would give it meaning. He had that writerly thing of never feeling solid enough about anything. Of being woozy about most things. Of course when you imagine you're in love with someone, all their faults feel like unique traits that give them character. It's disgusting how love can dumb you down. Anyway, what else do you want to know? So like I said, it would just make sense. He never would tell me what he was working on or what he did when he went out. He just shut me out after a while. Could you turn around, please. *(Beth has finished drying her hair and now selects a dress from the closet. She will proceed to put it on. Carl turns around.)* And then there was that quarrel we had soon after the attacks.

CARL. What quarrel would that be?

BETH. I almost flipped out because I thought he was actually gloating.

KHALED. That's enough, stop, stop, this is bullshit.

BARTLETT. *(Consulting notebook.)* That's the word she used: "gloating."

KHALED. I never "gloated," that's insane.

BARTLETT. *(Consulting notebook.)* She went on to say that she felt you were almost —

BARTLETT/BETH. Defending them.

BETH. Praising them even.

KHALED. That's a lie.

CARL. Are you sure about that?

BETH. It sure sounded like that to me.

KHALED. She's twisting everything.

BETH. *(To Carl.)* I don't think that would be an exaggeration.

KHALED. *(To Beth.)* That's not what I meant.

BETH. *(To Khaled.)* That's how it sounded. *(If light changes have been accompanying the transitions of time/new characters, a light change would also signal the shift here.)*

KHALED. I'm just saying we have to look for the "why"? Why did they do this?

BETH. Because they're evil assholes. Are you justifying this?

KHALED. Why are you so frightened of trying to figure this out?

BETH. Because if you go down that road then you're saying somewhere down the line there's a coherent argument for what they did. A legitimate reason. And there are some things that simply do not deserve the benefit of an explanation and being "enlightened" on an act like this would just be so fucking offensive. I don't want to know why they did this. I don't care.

KHALED. Don't you want to make sure it doesn't happen again? *(At some point, Khaled moves to help Beth zip up her dress, but she refuses his help. The exchange continues over this.)*

BETH. Next you'll tell me this is all our fault.

KHALED. Do you or do you not want to make sure this doesn't happen again?

BETH. And your solution is what, we should flagellate ourselves? It's not enough they fucked us over, now you want us to finish the job by beating ourselves up? Paralyze ourselves by examining our conscience?

KHALED. Our policies.

BETH. That's your idea of defense?

KHALED. We'll finish the job they started if we don't. You've always been able to see the bigger picture, why can't you see it now?

BETH. *(To Carl.)* It was more than what he was saying. It was an attitude. The way he looked. And I used to think we shared the same politics.

KHALED. *(To Bartlett.)* That is a complete — I wasn't justifying anything. I was saying let's get at the root causes so we can stop it once and for all. Where do you get "praising them" from that?

BETH. *(To Carl.)* There was almost like a gleam in his eye. Like he was saying, "it's just what you people deserve."

KHALED. *(To Beth.)* No.

BETH. *(To Khaled.)* You all but said it.

KHALED. Why aren't you hearing what I'm saying?

BETH. It was a rape, Khaled. It was a rape multiplied by a thousand. You don't go up to the woman who just got raped and say, you know what, I think you probably deserved that because you go around flaunting your ass so what do you expect. And if you want to make sure it doesn't happen again, then maybe you should go around in a fucking burqa.

KHALED. *(Disbelief, then:)* The United States of America is not a woman who just got raped. The United States of America is the biggest, strongest eight-hundred-pound gorilla on the block. *(Beth heads for the door.)* You can't rape an eight-hundred-pound gorilla, even if you wanted to. Where are you going? *(She doesn't answer.)* Beth. *(She starts to open the door but he shuts it.)* Where are you going?

BETH. You have a nerve. Like you tell me.

KHALED. I just want to know.

BETH. Why? Are you afraid I might say something to someone?

KHALED. What are you talking about? — Beth: Speak to me, you're freaking me out.

BETH. I followed you, you know.

KHALED. What?

BETH. Those times. When you went out. When you thought I was at work. *(To Carl.)* I should also tell you that I thought he was having an affair. I'm still not sure he wasn't. I think he was doing personals, or a chat room or something. Or that's what I thought. He certainly was at the computer a lot. It must have been something steamy because every time I approached him he would do something to hide the screen. *(Beth approaches Asfoor at the computer. Asfoor blocks the screen by turning around to face her. He smiles.)* Or he would turn it off. I became convinced he'd hooked up with someone. Met someone online. Our sex life ... well, never mind that. He denied it, of course. We had blow-ups about it. So ... one day, I followed him. I wanted an answer once and for all. So I followed him. To the park, where he met up with this woman ... It was strange. It didn't last long. He talked. She gave him something, then left. When I asked later what he'd done he said he'd been in all day working. The second time I followed him was the day I was to leave on a business trip. Only this time the person he met was a guy. *(Asfoor stands, goes to the closet, grabs a different hat and jacket, puts them on and waits at another point in the room.)* Again, it only lasted minutes. And it kind of weirded me out. Later I thought that was because I was thinking, oh no, Khaled's bi and we've been living a bigger lie than I thought. But it didn't have that vibe. Khaled looked almost — frightened. Once again it was quick. Khaled left first, then the guy. *(Asfoor exits through the front door.)* I left for my trip and told myself I'd deal with it later. Then the attacks happened and none of that mattered for a while. But when I confronted him he freaked out.

KHALED. *(To Beth.)* You've been what?

BETH. *(To Khaled.)* I called. You were never at home when you said you were supposed to be.

KHALED. You followed me? How dare you?

BETH. Don't turn this around, I'm fucking supporting you while you're supposed to be writing.

KHALED. That doesn't mean you own me.

BETH. Who were they, Khaled?

KHALED. Fuck you, no, it's none of your business.

BETH. I thought you were having an affair; but now I'm not so sure. Now I'm actually worried. With the things you've said in the past, and now, and these meetings, and your secrecy. Yes, I know you don't like to talk about what you're working on, only you've been working on it for as long as I've known you and you have nothing to show for it. Are you having an affair? Either you're having an affair or you're up to something you shouldn't be. Either one makes you a slimy little shit. So which is it? Tell me or I swear to God I will tell someone what I'm thinking.

KHALED. You can't be serious.

BETH. I am, I'm really wondering.

KHALED. Beth. It's me.

BETH. Great, now tell me who that is.

KHALED. We're all freaked out by what's happened. Don't flip out on me.

BETH. Why couldn't you be up to something? Why not? I'm not sure I even know you.

KHALED. Okay, stop.

BETH. I'm not sure I've ever known you.

KHALED. You're flipping out, stop it.

BETH. No, tell me. You don't talk about yourself or what you do. Your past is a fog. Suddenly you have material on subjects I had no idea you're interested in.

KHALED. What are you doing? This is like some fifties B movie, *I Married a Communist*.

BETH. Are you fucking around on me?

KHALED. No!

BETH. Then you must be up to something you shouldn't be and I'm really starting to freak out.

KHALED. *(Grabbing her.)* Would you just shut up? You can't talk like that. Not now. Not even for a joke, people take this shit very seriously. *(Beth just looks at him.)* Beth, Jesus Christ, wake up. I'm not a stranger.

BETH. *(To Carl, looking at Khaled.)* It's funny how people change on you. I mean normally, when you don't think you might be staring at a murderer. How you can be so fascinated and in love with someone and then find all that fall away. And the person stands there naked and butt ugly and you get angry at yourself for ever having wanted this man. I really hope these attacks haven't permanently spoilt my views on love.

KHALED. *(To Bartlett.)* It was a literary group.

BETH. *(To Carl.)* Imagine; that's what he said.

KHALED. For writers; to exchange ideas.

BETH. It was like watching a man hide himself in one box after another; like those Russian dolls.

KHALED. *(Still to Bartlett.)* I'm not joking, that's what it was.

BETH. I gave up after that. A few days later I asked him to move out.

CARL. Would you still have a picture of him?

BETH. I don't know; I can check.

CARL. I'd appreciate that. *(She exits. Carl makes notes.)*

KHALED. Jesus. No wonder you beat a path to my door. For God's sake. She has an ax to grind. It was a listserve for writers. We actually discussed plot lines and books. And yes, there was some flirting going on, so what; my moral behavior is not on trial here. And the guy was a jerk because he passed himself off as a woman online, and — he was just an asshole and I left. That's it. The sum total of my secrets. You could frame anything with enough menace and make it seem more than it is. *(Slight beat.)*

CARL. Bart.

BARTLETT. Yes, Carl.

CARL. Can I talk to you? *(Bartlett and Carl move off to talk in private. Carl speaks sotto voce throughout this next exchange.)*

BARTLETT. What?

CARL. Look: I'm thinking something.

BARTLETT. Go for it.

CARL. I don't think what we're doing now is getting us anywhere.

BARTLETT. Really? I feel like we're making headway.

CARL. Not — no.

BARTLETT. I think we've loosened his bowels and he's going to shit any second.

CARL. No, he's going to hold off because he's fixated on some idea of procedure. He thinks there's some script we're supposed to follow and that will protect him. He'll keep us a few facts shy of the truth and piss us off. The photo is too dark. And the clothes are generic. Important, but.

BARTLETT. The receipt is pretty damning.

CARL. We need him to spill his guts.

BARTLETT. What are you suggesting?

CARL. There's an imbalance of authority right now and we need to correct that.

BARTLETT. I tried that already and you pulled me off.

CARL. Yes. But with all due respect, I think I know these people a little better. I've been there. I know how they think. There's some dark shit you have to know how to access.

BARTLETT. Carl — we're not allowed to do that.

CARL. *(Gets out a small guidebook.)* Actually, if we don't hit any vital organs, we can.

BARTLETT. No, I don't think so.

CARL. *(Reading.)* "Section Eight, paragraph Two. Willful damage is not permitted but a relaxed, consistent pressure on parts of the body that may be deemed sensitive is allowed. As long as the suspect remains conscious and doesn't scream longer than ten seconds at any one time. Some bruising is allowed."

BARTLETT. *(Looks at the guidebook.)* Huh. I need to re-read this. I completely missed that.

CARL. It has surprisingly useful tips. Especially on how to use simple appliances like microwaves.

BARTLETT. You're suggesting what?

CARL. To bring the full weight of our authority to bear on him. With the aim of making him adjust his expectations as to what options are available to him. *(Slight beat.)*

BARTLETT. Fine … But gently.

CARL. Thanks. *(They turn to look at Khaled.)*

KHALED. What?

BARTLETT. *(To Carl.)* I'm going to use the john.

CARL. Take your time.

BARTLETT. *(To Khaled.)* Can I use your bathroom? — Thanks. *(Bartlett exits into the bathroom. Carl stares at Khaled.)*

KHALED. What's going on?

CARL. Khaled. *(Walks up to him.)* There's no easy way to segue into this. So I'm not going to try. *(Carl kicks Khaled in the groin. Khaled gasps, grabs his testicles, and collapses onto his knees.)* First off: That has been coming since we got here, because of repeated references to an innocence that is not yours to claim. If you were innocent, why would I have kicked you? Something you've done has given me good cause to assume the worst. The responsibility for that kick lies with your unwillingness to assume responsibility for the part we know you played. We need to know what that was. It might have been a bit part, but never think that makes you a bit player. *(Khaled doubles over and lets out a strangled cry.)* Khaled. — Khaled. *(Khaled topples over as he lets out a more sustained cry.)* Don't overdo it. I didn't hit you that hard. — That's not pain you're feeling, it's shock. You're overwhelmed by the notion of pain — that more might follow — not what I actually did. *(Khaled expresses more of his pain.)* Enough with the dramatics or I'll give you something to really scream about. *(Bartlett opens the bathroom door, looking concerned.)* It's nothing. We're good.

BARTLETT. What happened?

CARL. He's faking it.

KHALED. *(Strangled.)* No.

CARL. It's shock. I was abrupt.

BARTLETT. Over ten seconds.

CARL. But he's conscious and it wasn't a sustained cry.

KHALED. What are you doing?

BARTLETT. *(Worried.)* Carl.

CARL. It's under control. Go finish what you were doing.

BARTLETT. Absolutely no bones.

CARL. One more kick and I'm done.

BARTLETT. This has to lead to something.

CARL. The info is in the bag.

KHALED. *(Winded; to neighbors.)* Help. *(Bartlett gives Carl a worried look before going back into the bathroom. Khaled starts crawling towards the door.)* Help me.

CARL. If you'd've kept your nose clean, then you wouldn't be here, would you, crawling on the ground, trying to get away from the next hit that's sure to come if you don't tell us what you and Gamal got up to.

KHALED. Please.

CARL. We know you talked with him.

KHALED. No.

CARL. You met up. In the strip joint.

KHALED. I'm not hiding anything. I swear to you.

CARL. We have the receipt. It's as good as a photo.

KHALED. I don't know what you're talking about.

CARL. You really give a bad name to immigrants, you know that. Because of you we have to pass tougher laws that stop people who might actually be good for us.

KHALED. I haven't done anything wrong! *(Carl either kneels on Khaled's chest or else grabs him around the neck.)*

CARL. God: I know your type, so well. The smiling little Semite who gives you one face while trying to stab you with the other. You're pathetic, you know that. If you hate us, then just hate us. But you don't have the balls to do even that. You bitch and you moan and complain how overrun you are by us and all the time you can't wait to get here. You'd kill for a visa. That pisses me off. That's hypocrisy. Why not just come clean and own up that you hate everything this country stands for.

KHALED. *(Winded/strangled.)* No.

CARL. No, that's right, because you're too busy envying us.

KHALED. *(Winded/strangled.)* Get off me.

CARL. I could snap your neck just for that. What's the expression for "fuck-face" in Arabic? "Hitit khara"? "Sharmoot"?

KHALED. *(Winded/strangled.)* You're crushing me.

CARL. Just how crushed do you feel, Khaled? *(Slight beat, then:)* All right, I'm done. *(He lets go and stands up. Beat.)* Now do you want to tell me what you and Asfoor got up to in the strip club? Were you passing a message on to him? Were you the internet guy? The guy to help him get around? A carrier for something? What? What? Tell me, or I'll — *(Carl pulls his foot back as if to kick him.)*

KHALED. *(Flinching at threatened kick.)* No!

CARL. *(Continuing.)* I will. I'll exercise my drop kick on your testicle sack and make you sing an Arabic song in a very unnatural key.

KHALED. I'm going to be sick.

CARL. You're going to be sick. I'm the one who's throwing up. Only I have the decency to do it quietly, inside, and not make a public spectacle of myself. *(Perhaps grabbing Khaled by his lapels.)* What did he want from you? What did he want? What fucked-up part did you play in all of this? What happened with you in there? What happened when you met up with Asfoor? What did he want? *(Khaled opens his mouth as if he's about to vomit. Carl lets go as Khaled dry heaves. Slight beat.)* You know what I really resent? … What you force us to become. To protect ourselves. We are a decent bunch and do not want to be dragged down to your level. But no, you just have to drag us down, don't you. You have to gross us out with your level of crap. I personally hate this, you know that. I hate it when I have to beat the shit out of someone because then by an act of willful horror, whose effect on my soul I can only imagine, I have to shut out everything good about me to do my job to defend and protect. Here I am quickly devolving into a set of clichés I can barely stomach and you have the nerve to think you can vomit. No, it is I who am throwing up, sir, and if I see one scrap of food leave your mouth I will shove it back so far down your throat you'll be shitting it before you even know what you've swallowed again. *(Beth enters dressed in a coat now. She carries a photo.)*

BETH. I found this. *(Carl steps away from Khaled.)* It's pretty crumpled, but. I threw most of them out.

CARL. Thank you. *(He looks at photo.)* This will help.

BETH. Look — I … I just want to say … I have no idea if he was involved in anything. I know I've said things to suggest he might've been. But I'm just telling you what I thought at the time, when we were all upset. Being a major disappointment and a shit doesn't make you a criminal.

CARL. Understood.

BETH. Okay. — Good. — Just so I don't feel I'm — you know. — This isn't about revenge.

CARL. Believe it or not, safeguarding the innocent is as important as apprehending the bad guys.

BETH. Good. Okay. Well … Bye.

CARL. Thank you. *(She exits. As soon as the front door closes, the bathroom door opens and Bartlett enters. He walks over to Khaled, who is still prostrate on the ground.)*

BARTLETT. Anything?

CARL. He has a better idea of what's at stake.

BARTLETT. Anything solid?

CARL. Authority has been reestablished. That was important.

BARTLETT. Facts?

CARL. On the verge.

BARTLETT. Verge is where I left him.

CARL. Oh, I think he's ready to talk. I think he knows we're not looking for sequential sentences that add up to poop; but details that fit in nicely with what we know happened at the club. Where you went to get a hard-on while plotting death and destruction.

BARTLETT. Can we get him off the floor? It looks bad. *(Bartlett gets the chair as Carl moves to pick him up.)*

CARL. He's such a drama queen.

BARTLETT. *(Helps Carl pick up Khaled.)* The last piece of the puzzle fits, my friend. You were there. We had surveillance cameras. It wasn't your girlfriend who gave you away. It was your pecker.

(They sit him down.) You should have followed your religion's advice and avoided all depictions of the human form because that's what did you in.

CARL. Time for exhibit number four, I think.

BARTLETT. If we absolutely must.

CARL. You completely overlook her patriotism, you really do.

BARTLETT. I must have missed it. *(To Khaled.)* We'll tell you what happened and you just stop us if we have it wrong, okay? *(Throughout this next section, Khaled remains dazed, in shock. Carl will slide open both closet doors.)* On a Tuesday night, August twenty-first, at around 10:05, you went to the "EyeFull Tower Club"; where a Ms. Jean Sommers, aka, Kelly Cupid, "Dancer Extraordinaire and Stripper Artiste," as she calls herself, was performing. *(With the doors opened, a dancing pole is revealed. Light change in the closet to simulate club lighting. Perhaps a disco ball effect and a couple of spot lights. Jean Sommers is already at the pole. She is dressed for the act: elements of a cowboy outfit, including two pistols slung on each hip. She might also be wearing a wig.)* The date on your receipt proves it and so does Ms. Sommers.

JEAN. I do. Any way I can help, gentlemen.

CARL. Much appreciated.

JEAN. Will you want to see my act now?

BARTLETT. Is it relevant?

CARL. It might be. Clearly they met here for a reason. Your act may have been a signal of sorts. A series of unintended semaphores that spelt out a message to commence something. Why don't we have a look just to cover our bases.

JEAN. So you do want to see it?

CARL. You bet.

JEAN. You got it. Music. *(Appropriate music starts and she performs her act. More burlesque and pole dancing than striptease. After it ends, slight beat.)*

BARTLETT. I don't see how they could have passed messages through that.

CARL. Maybe not, but it doesn't hurt to check.

JEAN. That was the shortened version.

BARTLETT. When did you first notice him?

JEAN. The first time he came or the second?

CARL. Are we talking dates, or?

JEAN. *(Smiling.)* Yeah, dates.

BARTLETT. The first.

JEAN. Hardly at all. Except he was nervous and sweaty. Which isn't unusual when I come on. And he had a couple of books. I thought maybe he was a college grad trying to cram for an exam.

BARTLETT. Hardly a place to study.

JEAN. You'd be surprised. I see more and more people with laptops. We've begun to offer plug outlets in our lap-dance area.

BARTLETT. Anything else, that first time?

JEAN. Not really. I give full attention to my act. I believe in giving your best regardless of what you're doing.

CARL. It shows.

JEAN. Others leave their body when they do this, I don't. To me my body is a celebration of who I am and I give it to others as a revelation. I try to be your average Joe's desire incarnate. With a little extra thrown in for the more discerning. Nobody leaves my act feeling short-changed.

CARL. Kudos.

JEAN. Thanks.

BARTLETT. Anything else at first glance?

JEAN. No, he was just a set of eyes. It was later. When he asked for a lap dance that I had more time to observe him.

CARL. *(Showing her Khaled's photo.)* And you're sure it was this guy.

JEAN. Yeah, kinda. It was dark and he was wearing a baseball cap. But I'm pretty sure. And he was wearing this fatigue jacket. *(Bartlett picks up the baseball cap and fatigue jacket to show to Khaled.)*

BARTLETT. Any chance you remember the book titles?

JEAN. Yes, as a matter of fact. I'm always curious what other people are reading so I looked. One was on tattoos, and the other had something in the title — ending with God, which I thought was an odd combo. I plan on going back to college, you know.

BARTLETT. So what happened next? When you went one on one?

JEAN. Well … *(Moves towards Khaled. Appropriate music for a lap dance fades in quietly in the background.)* I began my routine. The usual. I was feeling less than on that day. I had been groped earlier and was not feeling well-disposed to the horny. But I do have a work ethic, like I said, and so I danced. I always give my best. *(She starts to sketch in some of her moves.)* Even to people who turn out later to be scum who want to do us harm. Did I tell you my father was a Marine?

CARL. No.

JEAN. Highly decorated. My outfit in many ways is a salute to him. That's what he was before he joined up. A cowboy, out west. At night, sometimes, he'd let me wear his medals.

BARTLETT. What can you tell us about Khaled?

JEAN. That's his name, huh?

BARTLETT. Yes.

JEAN. *(While dancing over a seated Khaled.)* If I had him again … I know what I'd do with him. Coming here to do that to us.

BARTLETT. Well, we don't know for sure if he's —

JEAN. *(Interrupting.)* I'd say touch me, Khaled, so the bouncers can come and smash your stupid face in. Coming here to get off on me while all the time wanting to do shit to us. Wrapping your women in black and then sneaking in here and getting your rocks off. I could pluck your eyes out. I could bend your dick round and fuck you up your own ass.

BARTLETT. Your sentiments are understandable. But if you could tell us what happened next.

JEAN. I should have known something was up. I thought he was extra sweaty because he was just too close to something he couldn't have. But it wasn't that. He was always looking around to check for something. It kinda pissed me off he wasn't giving me his full attention. At one time I stuck my boobs in his face and he actually moved his head, like I was blocking his view. I thought, what the hell are you doing here then? I take pride in what I do and expect some respect. Don't act like you're bored. I decided then and there to make him come. But then this guy shows up. Stands a few feet away and stares. Just stares. Like he'd paid for this show as well. "Do you mind?" I say to him.

BARTLETT. *(Shows her Asfoor's photo.)* This guy?

JEAN. Yeah. It was dark, but yeah. Both of them were Middle Eastern, that I know. So I tell him to piss off but he just stands there and this Khaled is looking at him. Suddenly his attention is full on him. And he's changed. Like he's frozen or something. And this guy just stares and he's looking at Khaled and me. And I say again, "Do you mind?" And he looks at me and his eyes — they're like, I'm-going-to-get-you eyes. Only they're smiling and it's creepy. And then he leaves to the restroom. And Khaled starts to rise like he wants to follow. Only I push him back down. I'm really pissed off at this point, like I've been insulted. Like my skills have been called into question. So I did something I never usually do. I reached down and squeezed. *(She does so.)* Just one time. And that did the trick. I finished him off. So easy … Then he springs out of that chair and into the restroom. *(The music stops; she moves away from Khaled.)* And that would have been it; I would have

47

moved on, onto the next customer, but something about them really annoyed me. So I looked for them to come out; to say something, like have some manners the next time, the both of you, and don't come back. But fifteen minutes later, they're still in there. And I say this to Stewart, one of the bouncers, and he says let me check, and I say, no, let me do it. If I can embarrass these guys I will, so I go in. *(She opens the bathroom door.)* And … *(A laugh.)* Damn if I don't see both of their legs under one of the stalls. And — they must have heard me, because Khaled comes shooting out and runs, just runs past me. And out saunters Mr. Creepy after him. Calm as can be, like he'd just been holding a meeting in his office. And I'm thinking — no, I actually say to him: "Take that shit somewhere else." And he stares at me again, and this time it's scary. Real scary. Like he's telling me he could snuff my life out with his pinkie if he wanted to. So I get out of there and tell Stewart about it, only they're both gone when he goes 'round to check … And that's my story.

BARTLETT. Did you get a sense of what they might have been doing in the stall?

JEAN. Not a clue. Might have been sucking each other off for all I know. Or shooting up. Who knows. At least one of them's dead. Have you got the other one yet?

CARL. We're working on it.

JEAN. I wouldn't mind getting him in that chair again. Give him a good thwack from me if you find him, care of Kelly Cupid.

CARL. Will do.

JEAN. Anything else I can do for you?

CARL. Not at the moment.

JEAN. Well … I'd better get ready for my act then.

CARL. Maybe we'll come back to check out the longer version.

JEAN. I'd like that. I'd hate to think my routine was being used for a nasty purpose. *(Jean smiles at Carl, then exits. Carl closes the closet doors. Bartlett and Carl turn to Khaled. Bartlett drags a chair and sits opposite Khaled. Carl either sits on the edge of the table, next to Khaled, or stands over him. Khaled looks at them. Beat.)*

KHALED. She's lying.

BARTLETT. Here's where I have to pry a little more than I like to. Can we — look at your pecker? Please? Very briefly. To clear something up. 'Cause this thing about tattoos keeps coming up. *(Khaled makes to bolt out of his chair, but Carl pins him down, wrapping his arms around his chest, immobilizing his arms. Bartlett puts on a latex glove.)* I'm sure it's nothing. I bet it's nothing. But it sure does make me wonder. *(Bartlett starts to undo Khaled's trousers. Khaled writhes in his chair in protest. This can be done with most of Khaled's back to the audience. Alternatively, this can take place on the futon, with the agents blocking most of the audience's view of Khaled.)*

KHALED. No. — No.

BARTLETT. *(Overlapping.)* What with that email he sent about tattoos, and the book, and doing it where the skin folds, where you can hide it.

KHALED. *(Half in tears.)* Stop it. No. — No.

BARTLETT. *(Overlapping.)* Was there like some secret mark you each showed yourselves? To ascertain something? Membership? Commitment? What were you doing in there for fifteen minutes? Excuse me. This is embarrassing for me too. *(He has yanked Khaled's pants down far enough for him to look.)* What's that? Is that a birthmark? Or? *(Carl also looks.)* What is that?

CARL. Liver spot?

BARTLETT. *(Still looking; slight beat.)* Yeah … Yeah. It's what it looks like … That couldn't be a tattoo, could it? … I wish we'd bought our camera with us … Next time. *(He continues to peer, then: a light slap on the thigh to indicate he's finished.)* All right. *(He stands.)* Thank you. Apologies for that. Not a part of the job that I like. *(Carl lets go, Khaled covers himself with his hands, and starts to pull up his trousers but Bartlett prevents him from doing so by placing his foot on his trousers.)* But it still leaves us wondering what you did all that time in the bathroom with one of the more hideous individuals we've come across? Now would be the time to fess up to any deviant sexual inclinations. It might get you off. *(Slight beat.)*

KHALED. *(Quiet.)* I was never there.

BARTLETT. *(Slight beat.)* All right … We're going to leave you to think about it. Come back later, tomorrow. We'll take a few things with us now. *(He nods to Carl to take the laptop.)* Look them over. Assess what we have. What needs filling in. — What might have occurred to you overnight. *(He picks up books from the pile.)* And then talk some more. You're not taking any long-distance trips, are you? *(Looks at Khaled, then moves to the door.)* Here're your choices, Khaled, that you can think about. Either you're innocent. In which case proving that might be difficult. Or you're guilty, in which case telling us now would score you points because we'll find out soon enough. Or: You're innocent of being guilty. You didn't know what you were getting into. Stumbled into it. Through deception. Other people's. Your own stupidity. And that would be okay too. We can work with that. We can work with you to make that seem plausible. *(At the door now. Carl carries the laptop.)* Think about it. And about those evaluation forms: They're no joke. It's your chance to respond. That's what this is all about. At the end of the day, we're fighting to safeguard that right. It sounds counter-intuitive. But that's the struggle for freedom for you. It's never as straightforward as you'd like it to be. *(Slight beat.)*

CARL. *(To Khaled.)* "Ma'salamma."

BARTLETT. *(Turns to Carl.)* What does that mean?

CARL. Peace be with you.

BARTLETT. I can go with that. *(To Khaled.)* Peace be with you. *(They take one last look at Khaled who remains slightly bent over, covering his crotch. They exit and close the door behind them. Beat. Khaled pulls up his trousers. Beat. The closet doors slide open revealing Asfoor. He enters the room.)*

ASFOOR. You … you help me, yes? You and me, private class. I have … I have need to — to learn. Quickly. Yes? … When first I come to this country — I not know how to speak. How … even to say anything. How one word best is placed with what word next. Yes? But in my head? It is a river of beautiful speech. Like in Arabic. Arabic is … It is the way into my heart. But everywhere, when I open ears, first thing, everywhere now, is English. You not get away from it. Even back home, before I come, I hear it more and more in people who do not speak it. I say, I must learn language that is everywhere. Language that has fallen on our heads and made us like — like children again. What is this power? What if I know it? I say to them, send me there so I learn this. I want to learn. And in my heart, I say I want to write. I want to write a book. In English. That is goal, yes? And one day, I say … *(While accent is maintained, the broken English gradually starts dropping.)* I might even teach it … I will teach language back. I will make them speak their own language differently. I will have them speak words they never spoke before. I will make them like children too, speaking words over and over to make sure they understand it. And soon my language will also fall on their heads. Like theirs falls on ours. Exploding in our brains 'til we can't even dream in peace. *(Slight beat.)* And so they sent me … They send me. *(Asfoor draws closer to Khaled. Khaled does not look at him.)* And now … my tongue … it wants to rise. Soar. As it used to. It wants to take off in this new language and conjure up brilliant words. It wants to do things in English that seemed so impossible for so long. I can help you find your voice too … You're stuck. I know you are. You've lost your way. I can feel it. I can help. Most of all … above all else, Khaled … I know how to inspire … I know how to inspire. *(Beat. Blackout.)*

End of Play

PROPERTY LIST

Books
Papers
Magazines
Laptop
Clothes
Picture frame
Music box
Passport
Form
Phone
Jacket with swizzle stick, receipt
Photos
Chair
Towel
Notebook, pen
Guidebook
Latex glove

SOUND EFFECTS

Toilet flushes

NEW PLAYS

★ **A DELICATE SHIP by Anna Ziegler.** A haunting love triangle triggers an unexpected chain of events in this poetic play. In the early stages of a new relationship, Sarah and Sam are lovers happily discovering each other. Sarah and Nate know everything about each other, best of friends since childhood and maybe something more. But when Nate shows up unannounced on Sarah's doorstep, she's left questioning what and who she wants in this humorous and heartbreaking look at love, memory, and the decisions that alter the course of our lives. "Ziegler (who makes origami of time)… digs beneath the laughs, of which there are plenty, to plumb the pain that lurks below." –*Time Out (NY)*. [2M, 1W] ISBN: 978-0-8222-3453-1

★ **HAND TO GOD by Robert Askins.** After the death of his father, meek Jason finds an outlet for his anxiety at the Christian Puppet Ministry, in the devoutly religious, relatively quiet small town of Cypress, Texas. Jason's complicated relationships with the town pastor, the school bully, the girl next door, and—most especially—his mother are thrown into upheaval when Jason's puppet, Tyrone, takes on a shocking and dangerously irreverent personality all its own. HAND TO GOD explores the startlingly fragile nature of faith, morality, and the ties that bind us. "HAND TO GOD is so ridiculously raunchy, irreverent and funny it's bound to leave you sore from laughing. Ah, hurts so good." –*NY Daily News*. [3M, 2W] ISBN: 978-0-8222-3292-6

★ **PLATONOV by Anton Chekhov, translated by John Christopher Jones.** PLATONOV is Chekhov's first play, and it went unproduced during his lifetime. Finding himself on a downward spiral fueled by lust and alcohol, Platonov proudly adopts as his motto "speak ill of everything." A shining example of the chaos that reigned in his era, Platonov is a Hamlet whose father was never murdered, a Don Juan who cheats on his wife and his mistress, and the hero of the as-yet unwritten great Russian novel of his day. [9M, 4W] ISBN: 978-0-8222-3343-5

★ **JUDY by Max Posner.** It's the winter of 2040, and the world has changed—but maybe not by much. Timothy's wife has just left him, and he isn't taking it well. His sisters, Tara and Kris, are trying to help him cope while wrestling with their own lives and loves. The three of them seem to spend a lot of time in their basements, and the kids are starting to ask questions. This subterranean comedy explores how one family hangs on when technology fails and communication breaks down. "This smart, disturbing comedy is set…just far enough in the future to be intriguingly weird but close enough to the present to be distressingly familiar… Posner's revelations about this brave new world… waver between the explicit and the mysterious, and each scene… gives us something funny and scary to ponder." –*The New Yorker*. [3M, 3W] ISBN: 978-0-8222-3462-3

DRAMATISTS PLAY SERVICE, INC.
440 Park Avenue South, New York, NY 10016 212-683-8960
postmaster@dramatists.com www.dramatists.com

NEW PLAYS

★ **PLACEBO by Melissa James Gibson.** A minty green pill—medication or sugar? Louise is working on a placebo-controlled study of a new female arousal drug. As her work in the lab navigates the blurry lines between perception and deception, the same questions pertain more and more to her life at home. With uncanny insight and unparalleled wit, Melissa James Gibson's affectionate comedy examines slippery truths and the power of crossed fingers. "Smart, droll, beautifully observed…" –*New York Magazine.* "… subtle yet intellectually explosive…" –*TheaterMania.com.* [2M, 2W] ISBN: 978-0-8222-3369-5

★ **THE ROAD TO DAMASCUS by Tom Dulack.** As full-scale civil war rages in Syria, a bomb explodes in Manhattan and all roads lead to Damascus. A peace-seeking African Pope is elected to the Vatican and an Evangelical third-party president is in power in the U.S. With nuclear war looming, will the new Pope intervene directly in American foreign policy, or will he accede to the demands of Washington? Riddled with international intrigue, Tom Dulack's astonishingly prescient play imagines a world ripped from today's headlines. "Serious… satisfying… This near-future tale of an ill-conceived American plan feels authentic enough to have you believe that such events could take place any day. Or to remind you that similar ones have already occurred." –*NY Times.* [5M, 2W] ISBN: 978-0-8222-3407-4

★ **FOUR PLACES by Joel Drake Johnson.** When Peggy's two adult children take her out for lunch, they quietly begin to take apart her life. The drinks come fast, the tempers peak, the food flies. "… a meticulously structured work that captures a decades-long history of paralyzing family resentments, depleted affections, and sublimated cruelties in a single, uninterrupted 90-minute scene." –*Chicago Reader.* "FOUR PLACES is intense, remorseless drama at its finest." –*Backstage.* [1M, 3W] ISBN: 978-0-8222-3448-7

★ **THE BIRDS by Conor McPherson, from a story by Daphne du Maurier.** The short story that inspired Alfred Hitchcock's classic film is boldly adapted by Conor McPherson—a gripping, unsettling, and moving look at human relationships in the face of societal collapse. In an isolated house, strangers Nat and Diane take shelter from relentless masses of attacking birds. They find relative sanctuary but not comfort or peace; there's no electricity, little food, and a nearby neighbor may still be alive and watching them. Another refugee, the young and attractive Julia, arrives with some news of the outside world, but her presence also brings discord. Their survival becomes even more doubtful when paranoia takes hold of the makeshift fortress—an internal threat to match that of the birds outside. "Deliciously chilling… spring-loaded with tension…" –*Irish Independent.* "[McPherson] keeps us on the edge of our seat." –*Irish Times.* [2M, 2W] ISBN: 978-0-8222-3312-1

DRAMATISTS PLAY SERVICE, INC.
440 Park Avenue South, New York, NY 10016   212-683-8960
postmaster@dramatists.com   www.dramatists.com

NEW PLAYS

★ **BUZZER by Tracey Scott Wilson.** Jackson, an upwardly-mobile black attorney, has just bought an apartment in a transitioning neighborhood in Brooklyn. He sees the potential of his old neighborhood, as does his white girlfriend Suzy… at first. When Jackson's childhood friend Don leaves rehab to crash with them, the trio quickly becomes trapped between the tensions inside their own home and the dangers that may lurk outside. "Skillful… [a] slow-burning, thought-provoking drama…" –*NY Times.* "[In BUZZER,] race is not a national conversation but an inner turmoil… the fact that the main gentrifier here is black turns the usual view of the subject inside out: Can one gentrify one's own home?" –*New York Magazine.* [3M, 1W] ISBN: 978-0-8222-3411-1

★ **THE NANCE by Douglas Carter Beane.** In the 1930s, burlesque impresarios welcomed the hilarious comics and musical parodies of vaudeville to their decidedly lowbrow niche. A headliner called "the nance"—usually played by a straight man—was a stereotypically camp homosexual and master of comic double entendre. THE NANCE recreates the naughty, raucous world of burlesque's heyday and tells the backstage story of Chauncey Miles and his fellow performers. At a time when it was easy to play gay and dangerous to be gay, Chauncey's uproarious antics on the stage stand out in marked contrast to his offstage life. "A nearly perfect work of dramatic art…" –*The New Yorker.* [4M, 4W] ISBN: 978-0-8222-3077-9

★ **EMPANADA LOCA by Aaron Mark.** Now living deep under Manhattan in an abandoned subway tunnel with the Mole People, a very hungry Dolores recounts her years selling weed with her boyfriend, her return to Washington Heights after thirteen years in prison, her fortuitous reunion with an old stoner friend who lets her give massages for cash in the basement under his empanada shop, and the bloodbath that sent her fleeing underground. Loosely inspired by the legend of Sweeney Todd, EMPANADA LOCA is contemporary Grand Guignol horror in the style of Spalding Gray. "Exuberantly macabre…" –*NY Times.* "Spine-tingling and stomach-churning…" –*Time Out (NY).* [1W] ISBN: 978-0-8222-3476-0

★ **SENSE OF AN ENDING by Ken Urban.** Charles, a discredited *New York Times* journalist, arrives in Rwanda for an exclusive interview with two Hutu nuns. Charged with alleged war crimes committed during the 1994 genocide, the nuns must convince the world of their innocence or face a lifetime in prison. When an unknown Tutsi survivor contradicts their story, Charles must choose which version of the truth to tell. Based on real events, SENSE OF AN ENDING shines a light on questions of guilt, complicity, and faith in the face of extreme violence. "A superb play… so intense that, in between each scene, you can hear the audience gulp for air." –*Time Out (London).* [3M, 2W] ISBN: 978-0-8222-3094-6

DRAMATISTS PLAY SERVICE, INC.
440 Park Avenue South, New York, NY 10016 212-683-8960
postmaster@dramatists.com www.dramatists.com

NEW PLAYS

★ **BETWEEN RIVERSIDE AND CRAZY by Stephen Adly Guirgis. Winner of the 2015 Pulitzer Prize.** Ex-cop and recent widower Walter "Pops" Washington and his newly paroled son Junior have spent a lifetime living between Riverside and crazy. But now, the NYPD is demanding his signature to close an outstanding lawsuit, the landlord wants him out, the liquor store is closed—and the church won't leave him alone. When the struggle to keep one of New York City's last great rent-stabilized apartments collides with old wounds, sketchy new houseguests, and a final ultimatum, it seems that the old days may be dead and gone. "Everyone's bound to be captivated by Guirgis's loudmouthed locals… [and] warm, rich dialect that comes right off the city streets." –*Variety.* [4M, 3W] ISBN: 978-0-8222-3340-4

★ **THE VEIL by Conor McPherson.** May 1822, rural Ireland. The defrocked Reverend Berkeley arrives at the crumbling former glory of Mount Prospect House to accompany a young woman to England. Seventeen-year-old Hannah is to be married off to a marquis in order to resolve the debts of her mother's estate. However, compelled by the strange voices that haunt his beautiful young charge and a fascination with the psychic current that pervades the house, Berkeley proposes a séance, the consequences of which are catastrophic. "… an effective mixture of dark comedy and suspense." –*Telegraph (London).* "A cracking fireside tale of haunting and decay." –*Times (London).* [3M, 5W] ISBN: 978-0-8222-3313-8

★ **ASHVILLE by Lucy Thurber.** Chronologically the second play in Lucy Thurber's The Hill Town Plays cycle, ASHVILLE is the story of Celia, sixteen years old and trapped in her poor white rural town, among people who can't hope for anything more than a good blue-collar job and a decent marriage. Celia wants something else in life, even if she can't articulate what that is. For a fleeting moment she thinks she finds the unnameable thing in her neighbor and tentative friend Amanda, but it may be that no one else can save Celia—only she herself can orchestrate her escape. "The best thing about these five plays is the detailed and quite devastating portrait they present of the depressed industrial region of western Massachusetts…" –*Variety.* [4M, 3W] ISBN: 978-0-8222-3355-8

★ **DOV AND ALI by Anna Ziegler.** Once upon a time, in the middle of a school, in the middle of Detroit, in the middle of the United States of America, there was a confused teacher and a precocious student. When Dov, an orthodox Jew, and Ali, a strict Muslim, get caught in a cultural crossfire, both are confronted with the same choice: Will they stand by their beliefs or face the devastating consequences? "… a flawless play… In a time of ceaseless snark and cynicism, its earnestness in asking bigger questions can be downright refreshing." –*NY Times.* "… an intense, intelligent and hugely promising play…" –*Guardian (UK).* [2M, 2W] ISBN: 978-0-8222-3455-5

DRAMATISTS PLAY SERVICE, INC.
440 Park Avenue South, New York, NY 10016 212-683-8960
postmaster@dramatists.com www.dramatists.com

NEW PLAYS

★ **EMERGING ARTIST GRANT by Angus MacLachlan.** Ethan, a successful independent filmmaker, is sweating over casting his newest project in his hometown of Winston-Salem when Spencer, a newly-minted adjunct theatre professor, auditions for the lead. Their mutual attraction is immediate, and they start a charming and amusing dance of personal and professional eroticism. Ethan's smart and witty older sister, Liz, is thrown into the mix. She supports herself as a hairdresser; her acting career, and her hopes, have derailed a bit with time. A subtly comedic story set in the creative world, EMERGING ARTIST GRANT explores how we struggle to make something of our lives, and it questions the moral crises we encounter when trying for our dreams. "… [A] witty play [and] something of a master class in artistic self-appraisal and survival… the questions of how many interpersonal boundaries are transgressed… remain up in the air until the end." *–IndyWeek.com.* [1M, 2W] ISBN: 978-0-8222-3365-7

★ **THE BELLE OF AMHERST by William Luce.** In her Amherst, Massachusetts, home, the reclusive nineteenth-century poet Emily Dickinson recollects her past through her work, her diaries and letters, and a few encounters with significant people in her life. "William Luce has chiseled a perfectly detailed cameo… He has made an Emily so warm, human, loving and lovable that her ultimate vulnerability will break your heart." *–Boston Globe.* [1W] ISBN: 978-0-8222-3373-2

★ **LET ME DOWN EASY by Anna Deavere Smith.** In this solo show constructed from verbatim interview transcripts, Anna Deavere Smith examines the miracle of human resilience through the lens of the national debate on health care. After collecting interviews with over 300 people on three continents, Smith creates an indelible gallery of 20 individuals, known and unknown—from a rodeo bull rider and a World Heavyweight boxing champion to a New Orleans doctor during Hurricane Katrina, as well as former Texas Governor Ann Richards, cyclist Lance Armstrong, film critic Joel Siegel, and supermodel Lauren Hutton. A work of emotional brilliance and political substance from one of the treasures of the American theater. Originally created as a one-person show, the author encourages multi-actor productions of the play. "It's stunning, beautiful, and transcendent." *–SF Weekly.* [1W] ISBN: 978-0-8222-2948-3

★ **PORT AUTHORITY by Conor McPherson.** PORT AUTHORITY follows three generations of Irishmen as they tell the stories of their lives. "Overwhelmingly poignant…McPherson rivetingly shows how the past is in all our presents." –Evening Standard (London). "McPherson occupies his familiar terrain with glittering wit and assurance… he writes like a recording Irish angel…[with] a poetic understanding of what might have been." *–Guardian (UK).* [3M] ISBN: 978-0-8222-3311-4

DRAMATISTS PLAY SERVICE, INC.
440 Park Avenue South, New York, NY 10016 212-683-8960
postmaster@dramatists.com www.dramatists.com

NEW PLAYS

★ **BRIGHT HALF LIFE by Tanya Barfield.** A moving love story that spans decades in an instant—from marriage, children, skydiving, and the infinite moments that make a life together. "BRIGHT HALF LIFE, a sixty-five minute chronicle of a deeply committed lesbian relationship, is contemporary as a play could be but the theme is classic and timeless… the presentation of the highs and lows of coupledom, as exampled in this piece, defy the ages." –*Huffington Post.* [2W] ISBN: 978-0-8222-3351-0

★ **WAIT UNTIL DARK by Frederick Knott, adapted by Jeffrey Hatcher.** Forty-seven years after *Wait Until Dark* premiered on Broadway, Jeffrey Hatcher has adapted Frederick Knott's 1966 original, giving it a new setting. In 1944 Greenwich Village, Susan Hendrix, a blind yet capable woman, is imperiled by a trio of men in her own apartment. As the climax builds, Susan discovers that her blindness just might be the key to her escape, but she and her tormentors must wait until dark to play out this classic thriller's chilling conclusion. "… reminds CGI-infected audiences that a few shadows, a shiny knife, and compelling characters can still go a long way to create suspense… WAIT UNTIL DARK earns its climax through enthralling, layered characters." –*Entertainment Weekly.* [4M, 2W] ISBN: 978-0-8222-3205-6

★ **BAKERSFIELD MIST by Stephen Sachs.** Maude, a fifty-something un-employed bartender living in a trailer park, has bought a painting for a few bucks from a thrift store. Despite almost trashing it, she's now convinced it's a lost masterpiece by Jackson Pollock worth millions. But when world-class art expert Lionel Percy flies over from New York and arrives at her trailer home in Bakersfield to authenticate the painting, he has no idea what he is about to discover. Inspired by true events, this hilarious and thought-provoking new comedy-drama asks vital questions about what makes art and people truly authentic. "A triumph! Hugely gratifying! An absorbing, hilarious two-hander about the nature of art and the vagaries of human perception." –*Backstage.* "Sachs' short, clever play is a battle of wits." –*NY Times.* [1M, 1W] ISBN: 978-0-8222-3280-3

★ **SWITZERLAND by Joanna Murray-Smith.** Somewhere in the Swiss Alps, grande dame of crime literature Patricia Highsmith lives with an impressive collection of books, and a somewhat sinister collection of guns and knives. She finds solace in her solitude, her cats, and cigarettes. But when a mysterious international visitor arrives at her perfectly secluded home, her love of fictional murders becomes a dangerous reality. "[SWITZERLAND] explores what it's like to be a woman writer in a man's literary kingdom… Murray-Smith's dialogue sparkles with witty one-liners and delicious snark…" –*Time Out (Sydney).* [1M, 1W] ISBN: 978-0-8222-3435-7

DRAMATISTS PLAY SERVICE, INC.
440 Park Avenue South, New York, NY 10016 212-683-8960
postmaster@dramatists.com www.dramatists.com